ARE WE ALMOST THERE?

The Kid's Book of Travel Fun

Annette LaPlaca

illustrated by Debbie Bryer

Harold Shaw Publishers
Wheaton, Illinois

For Angie, Jenny, and Jessica

"God's Good Creation," p.14, © 1992 by Joyce Heinrich, is reprinted with permission of the author.

Scripture is taken from *The Holy Bible: New International Version.* Copyright 1973, 1978, 1984 by the International Bible Society. Used by permission of Zondervan Publishing House.

Copyright © 1992 by Harold Shaw Publishers

Inside art © 1992 by Debbie Bryer

Cover art and design by David LaPlaca

ISBN 0-87788-051-4

Ready!
Get Set!
Go!

They love to visit new places. Sam, their pet salamander, always tags along. He likes to have his picture taken. Look for him on every page. Sam, Suzy, and Leon can't wait to take this trip with you!

Taking a trip means it's time for adventure!

It's always exciting to explore God's big world. What new places will you see? What new people will you meet? What kind of fun is just down the road?

What are the names of the city and state where you live?

_____

Where are you going on this trip?
(This may be more than one place.)

_____

_____

_____

Who will go with you on this trip? Make a list here.

_____   _____

_____   _____

_____   _____

Before you start, say this prayer with the other travelers in your car:
    Dear God,

        Thank you for creating a world full of different people and places to enjoy. Thank you that we can begin this adventure. Keep us safe as we go. We love you!

A promise from God's Word:

    Be strong and courageous . . . for the LORD your God will be with you wherever you go. Joshua 1:9

What to Take in the Car

What important items will you pack in your backpack or travel bag? Unscramble these words to make a list of things you might take along in the car. The first letter of each word will help you get started.

1. psma	1. m a p s
2. rppea	2. p _ _ _ _
3. yroacsn	3. c _ _ _ _ _ _
4. kosbo	4. b _ _ _ _
5. lcnepis	5. p _ _ _ _ _ _
6. areggab gba	6. g _ _ _ _ _ _ _ _ _
7. cssakn	7. s _ _ _ _ _
8. ysto	8. t _ _ _
9. simuc	9. m _ _ _ _
10. liwolp	10. p _ _ _ _ _
11. ulssssaegn	11. s _ _ _ _ _ _ _ _ _
12. liBbl	12. B _ _ _ _
13. kdce fo sracd	13. d _ _ _ _ _ _ _ _ _ _
14. ootboenk	14. n _ _ _ _ _ _ _
15. aearmc	15. c _ _ _ _ _

A riddle for you:

What's harder than following a road map? _____

Answers are on page 44.

At the Beach

Snorkeling is swimming with your face underwater, using a mask and a breathing tube to discover the mysterious things that go on under the surface of the sea. God gave certain plants and animals a home there. Use your imagination to color their home under the sea!

The Maker of heaven and earth, the sea, and everything in them— the LORD, who remains faithful forever. Psalm 146:6

On the Road Again
Super Search

Search for these words about car travel and circle them. Be ready to read up and down, sideways, backwards, and diagonally!

accelerator
backing up
brakes
bridge
car
construction
deer crossing
driving

east
exit
fast food
flat tire
forward
freeway
gas stations

gears
highway
hotels
interstate
miles per hour
motels
no passing zone
north

odometer
off ramp
on ramp
policemen
railroad crossing
rest area
reverse
route
seatbelt
semi-truck
south
spare tire
speedometer
speed limit
stop
stoplight
street lights
toll booth
traffic jam
truck stop
turnpike
weigh station
west
white stripes
yellow stripes
yield

```
T R A F F I C J A M I N T E R S T A T E
O U V E O L H C O L S I S O T P L N N T
L I R G W N A T H S E K A R B G V O U U
L H G N Y U E T S R E V E R S E Z R H O
B Y E E P L R S T V T E C A R G K T B R
O I A X S I A H U I T A E Z N S O H R E
O N R T M B K T X L R Y B I F E D W I X
T U S L R F C E I S S E S R H M O A D G
H O T E L S Y G A T P S I E A I M M G N
T R I B G E H P Q O A D N T C T E I E I
J E M T A T D U U P R R E E C R T L I S
O S I A S O R G O L E H M M E U E E G S
N T L E S N C N S I T I E O L C R S E O
S A D S T O P I J G I G C D E K F P W R
E R E K A I A K E H R H I E R U I E E C
P E E P T T P C E T E W L E A R Y R I R
I A P O I C D A B Y P A O P T E A H G E
R M S T O U O B A O N Y P S O T W O H E
T L E S N R Y W R B F M W M R J E U S D
S S X K S T S I X G A O B J A D E R T R
E O Q C N S W P E R L M H L C R R G A I
T U M U E N A C N L D R A W R O F K T V
I T L R Q O R O E Z D O D F T S A F I I
H H X T K C Q Y Z A A B X H E C O A O N
W E S T R A I L R O A D C R O S S I N G
```

5

Answers are on page 44.

Take It Along Crossword

What should you take along when you travel? Use the clues to help you fill in the blanks across and down with the right words. You'll find answers on page 44. But no peeking until you're done!

ACROSS

1. To protect from wind and rain
3. To play in the car
5. Entertainment with notes and melody
7. For carrying everything
9. Denim pants for all adventures
10. For seeing in the dark
12. Soft and fluffy for your head
13. For running, jumping feet
14. Things to play with

DOWN

1. To take pictures with
2. To keep the raindrops off your head
4. For knowing where you're going
6. Shade for your eyes
8. Fun reading with pictures
11. For munching in the car

Answers are on page 44.

God Created You

What makes you just the way you are, like no one else in the world? Who made you? The Bible tells us the answers to questions like that.

So God created man in his own image, in the image of God he created him; male and female he created them. . . . God saw all that he had made, and it was very good. Genesis 1:27, 31

Who made people? _____

What two types of people are there? _____ _____

What did God say about the people he created?_____

For you created my inmost being;
*   you knit me together in my mother's womb.*
I praise you because I am fearfully and wonderfully made;
*   your works are wonderful, I know that full well. . . .*
How precious to me are your thoughts, O God! Psalm 139:13-14, 17

These verses say that God created you, inside and out! And it says that God's work in creating people was "wonderful!" Write down three things about yourself that you think are wonderful (for example: I'm good at football, I'm nice to my brother).

_____

_____

_____

The last line of this verse says, "How precious to me are your thoughts, O God!" The person who wrote this is glad that God is thinking of him. Isn't it good to know that God is thinking of you and caring for you?

Say thank you to God:

Dear God, thank you for making me just the way I am. Thank you for making me_____, _____,and _____ (name the three things on your list). Thank you for thinking of me and caring for me. You are a loving God!

Rules of the Road

As you see these signs along the road, draw a picture of the shape and letters of each sign. You can draw other signs you see that aren't listed here, too.

STOP SIGN	SPEED LIMIT SIGN
YIELD SIGN	TRAFFIC STOPLIGHT
RAILROAD CROSSING	STREET NAME SIGN
DEER CROSSING	NO PASSING
ONE WAY	ROAD CONSTRUCTION

God Made, People Made

God is the Creator of the whole earth—and of you! The Bible says that when God created people, he made them "in his image"—which means that people are creative, too. Look around you. What do you see? You see some things that God made and some things that people made by using the creative minds that God gave them. By looking at the things outside your car windows, fill in two lists—things God made and things people made.

THINGS GOD MADE

1. _____
2. _____
3. _____
4. _____
5. _____
6. _____
7. _____
8. _____
9. _____
10. _____

THINGS PEOPLE MADE

1. _____
2. _____
3. _____
4. _____
5. _____
6. _____
7. _____
8. _____
9. _____
10. _____

God saw all that he had made, and it was very good. Genesis 1:31

Pray

Thank you, God, for making _____ (name the things on your first list). And thank you for giving me a creative mind and an imagination. Thank you for making people "in your image."

Who Am I?

A Guessing Game

Here's a game you can play with one or more of the others traveling with you. The person holding the book (maybe you!) gets to be the clue-giver. Give one clue, then give each of the other players a chance to make a guess. If no one guesses the answer, give the second clue. Give every player another chance to guess. Keep going until someone guesses the answer, or you run out of clues.

Answers are on page 44.

1. Who Am I?

Clue #1: I work outdoors in all kinds of weather.
Clue #2: Sometimes I wear bright orange so people can see me.
Clue #3: In my job I work with cement and blacktop.
Clue #4: When I'm working cars speed past me.

2. Who Am I?

Clue #1: In my job, I sit down and go forward at the same time.
Clue #2: My job helps other people travel.
Clue #3: Monday through Friday, I see lots of kids going to school.
Clue #4: My vehicle is usually bright yellow.

3. Who Am I?

Clue #1: I wear a uniform to do my job.
Clue #2: Sometimes I work at night because people need my help at all times of the day.
Clue #3: To get my job, I had to learn all about the human body and other sciences.
Clue #4: Usually I work with people who are sick or hurt.

4. Who Am I?

Clue #1: It would be easy to get fat doing my job!
Clue #2: In my job, I use lots of flour, sugar, and eggs.
Clue #3: My work area is usually very warm because of the ovens.
Clue #4: My work goes from my big kitchen to provide many people with goodies for breakfast or bread for their lunchtime sandwiches.

Pray

Thank you, God, for making all kinds of different people and different kinds of jobs. Thank you for making a world so full of things to do!

Super Scavenger Hunt

On a scavenger hunt, the players collect odd items and then come together to see which players collected the most items from the list. You can collect these "sights" on your own or with the other travelers in your car, or you can race with another traveler to see who collects the most items on your trip. Put your initials in the blanks to show when you've collected a "sight."

____ a river
____ a truck driver who will wave or honk
      for you
____ 3 different gas stations (name them)

_____

_____

_____

____ a horse
____ a station wagon with kids in the car
____ a farmer's fields
____ a fast-food restaurant (name it)

_____

____ a boat
____ a rest area
____ any car with skis, bikes, or luggage
      attached on the outside

____ a purple car or truck
____ a hotel, motel, or inn (name it)

_____

____ raindrops on the windshield of your
      car
____ license plates for four different states
      (name them)

_____

_____

_____

_____

____ a police car
____ cows
____ a person riding a bicycle
____ a bus full of travelers
____ an airplane or helicopter

How many items did you find?

10-15 You're a hard-working watcher!
16-20 You're an excellent observer!
21-25 You're a Super Scavenger!

11

A-B-C!

Knowing the alphabet can help you have lots of travel fun—either all by yourself or with the other travelers in the car.

By yourself:

Search outside the windows of your car for the letters of the alphabet. You have to find the letters in order. You might discover an "A" in a billboard, a "B" in a road sign, and a "C" in another car's license plate. Don't feel bad if you get stuck on "Q" or "Z"—after a while you can skip those and finish the list.

All together:

Split the car travelers into two teams (or play with one other person). The travelers on each side of the car should search for the alphabet letters in order. If both teams are searching for the same letter, such as "J," and one side sees it first, they get to count it and move on to "L." The other team must keep looking for a "J" of their own. The first team to make it to "Z" are the A-B-C champs!

Make a List

Using the spaces provided below, fill in things you see around you—in your car or out the windows—that begin with the letters of the alphabet. You don't need to go in order. You might see a river right now and a balloon in half an hour.

You might fill the blanks like this:

A _____   N _____
B _____   O _____

Try it yourself!

A _____   H _____   N _____   T _____
B _____   I _____   O _____   U _____
C _____   J _____   P _____   V _____
D _____   K _____   Q _____   W _____
E _____   L _____   R _____   X _____
F _____   M _____   S _____   Y _____
G _____   Z _____

I Went to the Store, and I Bought _____!

With the other travelers in your car (or at least with one other person), take turns finishing this sentence. Get ready to put your memory to work!

Player #1 fills in the blank with an item beginning with the letter "A":

I went to the store, and I bought Apples.

Player #2 adds to this with an item beginning with "B":

I went to the store, and I bought Apples and Bananas.

Take turns among the travelers in your car. Your list can grow long:

I went to the store, and I bought Apples, Bananas, Cupcakes, Dogfood, Eggs, Fish, and Grapes.

When a player makes a mistake by forgetting or getting the items out of order, that player must drop out. The last player in the game is the Memory Champ!

Other list ideas are:

I went to the zoo, and there were _____.

I looked in my closet, and I found _____.

I took a trip around the world, and I saw _____.

God's Good Creation

Everywhere I go
This is what I see . . .
God's small creation
Looking up at me.

Little fragrant flowers,
Violets, bluebells.
Funny fish and birds,
Pebbles and seashells.

Everywhere I go
This is what I see . . .
God's big creation
Looking down at me.

Elephants and whales,
Trees and hills so high.
Big rocks and islands,
Clouds across the sky.

Everywhere I go
This is what I see . . .
God's great creation
In front and back of me.

Huge, towering mountains,
Waves and rolling seas.
Sparkling stars and moon,
Winds and blowing breeze.

I look in the mirror,
This is what I see . . .
God's best creation
Looking back at me!

Curly hair like Mom.
Bright eyes like my dad.
God planned and made me
To love him—I'm glad!

Joyce Heinrich

Sing, Sing a Song!

Together with the other travelers in your car, sing as many songs as you can think of that contain the words from the list below. For the word "yellow," you might sing "The Yellow Rose of Texas," "Tie a Yellow Ribbon," and "We All Live in a Yellow Submarine." Keep thinking of songs until no one can think of another. Then move on to the next word on the list. You'll be surprised at how many songs you know!

How many songs can you sing for each of the words listed here?

BLUE
SEA
AMERICA
DREAM
HORSE
BABY
FLAG
SLEEP
SING
JINGLE
HAPPY
NIGHT

Sing to the LORD a new song, for he has done marvelous things. Psalm 98:1
With singing lips my mouth will praise you. Psalm 63:5

What kind of music do fathers sing in the car?_____

Answer is on page 44.

Pick a Flower!

Aren't you glad that God didn't make everything in his creation blue? Or everything red? Thank him for coloring his world full of bright colors! Every state in the United States has chosen a certain flower to be its state flower. Some of them are on this page, waiting for you to color them!

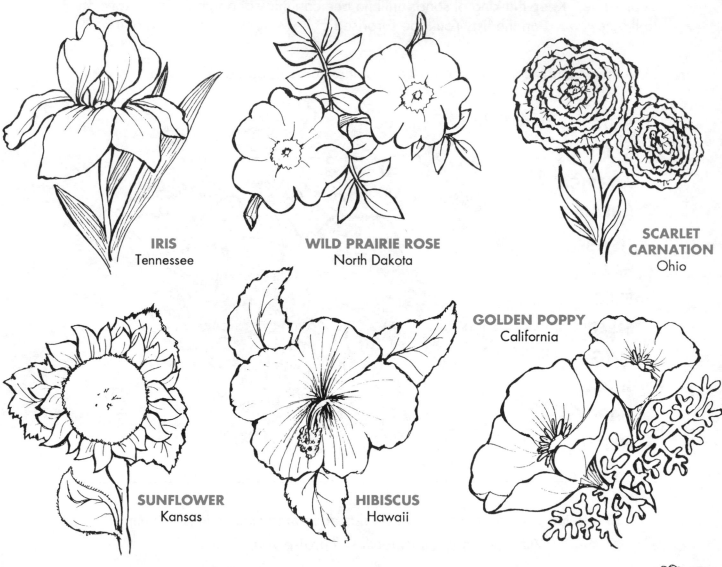

IRIS
Tennessee

WILD PRAIRIE ROSE
North Dakota

SCARLET CARNATION
Ohio

SUNFLOWER
Kansas

HIBISCUS
Hawaii

GOLDEN POPPY
California

Say Thank You to God

Dear God, thank you for making your world so beautiful. Thank you especially for creating colors and shapes for our eyes to enjoy. You are a great artist, God!

16

God, the Provider

Our Creator God made the world, and he takes good care of it. Read these verses and make a list of the things, animals, or people that God provides for (for example, "wild donkeys").

He makes springs pour water into the ravines;
* it flows between the mountains.*
They give water to all the beasts of the field;
* the wild donkeys quench their thirst.*
The birds of the air nest by the waters;
* they sing among the branches.*
He waters the mountains from his upper chambers;
* the earth is satisfied by the fruit of his work.*
He makes grass grow for the cattle,
* and plants for man to cultivate—*
* bringing forth food from the earth.*
Psalm 104:10-14

_____
_____
_____
_____
_____
_____
_____
_____

Answers are on page 44.

Do you ever worry that you won't have enough to eat or clothes to wear? God says to look at how well he cares for birds and other animals and remember that you are much more important to him.

Look at the birds of the air; they do not sow or reap or store away in barns, and yet your heavenly Father feeds them. Are you not much more valuable than they? . . . Seek first his kingdom and his righteousness, and all these things will be given to you as well.
Matthew 6:26, 33

Write down six things that God has given you.

_____
_____
_____
_____
_____
_____

Every good and perfect gift is from above, coming down from the Father of the heavenly lights, who does not change like shifting shadows. James 1:17

This verse says that every good thing we have comes from God. Take time out to say thank you to God for each of the six things that you wrote down.

What Do You See?

Turn the lines in each square into a picture all your own. Use your imagination!

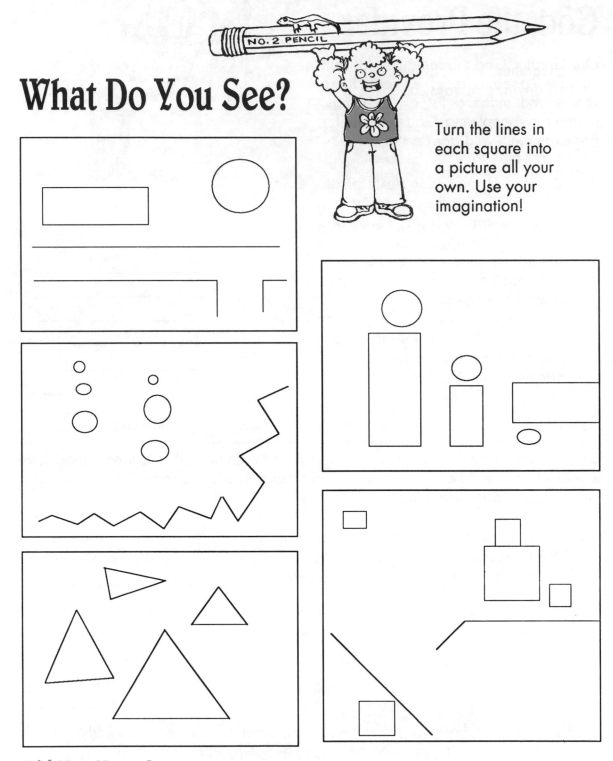

Did You Know?

Did you know that no two people are just alike? God made each person unique—one-of-a-kind. No one has a personality or imagination like yours.

Take a Trip Super Search

Search for these words about traveling or vacations and circle them. Be ready to read up and down, sideways, backwards, and diagonally!

adventure
airplane
amusement park
attractions
automobile
backpack
beach
boat
bus
camera
camper
camping
car
cruise
drive
excursion
explore
forest
freeway
highway
hiking
holiday
horseback riding
journey
mileage
mountains
national park
ocean
recreation
relaxation
resort
rest stop
roads
route
safety
sleeping bag
sports
state park

suitcase
sunglasses
tent
tour

tourist
trailer
train
travel

vacation
voyage
walking
weather

```
B  U  S  D  W  R  U  O  T  C  S  E  S  S  A  L  G  N  U  S
O  B  A  E  H  E  S  L  E  E  P  I  N  G  B  A  G  A  G  F
A  I  M  L  O  Y  A  W  H  G  I  H  P  N  Y  C  S  T  V  J
T  A  T  T  R  A  C  T  I  O  N  S  K  O  N  A  Q  I  R  K
R  R  I  S  W  Z  B  D  H  P  L  S  U  I  L  M  E  O  A  R
B  R  I  T  A  C  A  E  R  E  S  T  S  T  O  P  R  N  L  A
G  N  I  P  M  A  C  F  E  S  R  L  O  A  R  E  U  A  D  P
K  N  W  I  O  L  K  H  R  A  M  P  I  C  A  R  T  L  H  T
F  A  N  N  U  S  P  O  O  C  I  E  X  A  M  I  N  P  I  N
M  E  L  O  N  C  A  R  L  T  T  R  A  V  E  L  E  A  J  E
F  C  U  I  T  O  C  S  P  I  R  A  P  U  O  L  V  R  O  M
R  O  A  T  A  S  K  E  X  U  T  N  A  L  E  Y  D  K  U  E
E  R  R  A  I  B  N  B  E  S  I  U  R  C  A  K  A  O  R  S
E  R  E  E  N  A  I  A  P  H  S  Y  E  U  T  N  H  G  N  U
W  E  M  R  S  Y  H  C  I  A  N  E  T  L  L  E  E  L  E  M
A  J  A  C  T  T  A  K  H  T  V  O  S  H  I  N  E  T  Y  A
Y  H  C  E  E  G  I  R  L  I  M  K  I  R  E  L  I  A  R  T
A  M  F  R  E  N  D  I  R  O  I  R  R  T  W  A  D  I  L  R
C  A  A  J  G  Y  O  D  B  A  L  A  U  P  A  C  V  G  O  A
S  E  X  C  U  R  S  I  O  N  E  P  O  A  L  X  N  A  P  I
P  U  L  I  L  X  L  N  T  I  A  E  T  M  K  N  A  I  A  N
O  Y  M  A  U  E  C  G  E  P  G  T  O  A  I  E  T  L  B  K
R  E  O  M  Y  R  I  B  A  L  E  A  N  E  N  S  N  T  E  G
T  M  V  B  E  A  C  H  V  N  L  T  L  R  G  E  T  U  O  R
S  S  D  A  O  R  N  E  T  O  T  S  U  Y  A  D  I  L  O  H
```

Answers are on page 44.

19

How Many?

Look around your car to discover the numbers that fill in these blanks.

1. How many travelers are in your car? (You can count people and pets.) _____

2. How many miles are on the mileage meter right now? (Ask the driver.) _____

3. How many tires are ON or IN your car? _____

4. How many mirrors are ON or IN your car? _____

5. How many seatbelts are there in your car? _____
   How many people are using their seatbelts? _____

6. How many windows are there in your car? _____

7. What time is it? (If there is no clock in your car, ask a person who has a watch.) _____

8. How many pedals are there on the floor on the driver's side of the car? _____

9. How many doors are there in your car? _____

10. How many keys are on your driver's keychain? _____

11. How many buttons or knobs work your car's radio? _____

12. How fast is your car going now? _____ miles per hour. What is the highest speed marked on your car's speedometer? _____ (Be sure not to go that fast!)

A Riddle for You
What ten-letter word starts with g-a-s? _____

Answer is on page 44.

Match Them Up!

These vacation-time ACTIVITIES need to be matched up to the PLACES where you might do them. Draw lines to match ACTIVITIES to PLACES. Be careful, though! Some activities, such as "swimming," can be done in more than one place.

sandcastle building
flying kites
waterskiing
sledding
camping
feeding seagulls
rollerskating
surfing
whale-watching
jogging
swimming
fishing
ferris-wheel riding
shell collecting
snorkeling
picnicking
rollercoaster riding
hiking
boating
diving
merry-go-round riding

LAKE

MOUNTAINS/WOODS

OCEAN/BEACH

AMUSEMENT PARK

Answers are on pages 44-45.

A Question for You:

Which of these activities have you done? Put an "X" beside the ones you've enjoyed!

The United States of America

50 States Super Crossword

Using the clues, fill in the blanks across and down with the names of the fifty states. The state names are listed to help you spell the words perfectly! (You won't use them all).

Alabama
Alaska
Arizona
Arkansas
California
Colorado
Connecticut
Delaware
Florida
Georgia
Hawaii
Idaho
Illinois
Indiana
Iowa
Kansas
Kentucky
Louisiana
Maine
Maryland
Massachusetts
Michigan
Minnesota
Mississippi
Missouri
Montana
Nebraska
Nevada
New Hampshire
New Jersey
New Mexico
New York
North Carolina
North Dakota
Ohio
Oklahoma
Oregon
Pennsylvania
Rhode Island
South Carolina
South Dakota
Tennessee
Texas

Utah
Vermont
Virginia
Washington
Wisconsin
West Virginia
Wyoming

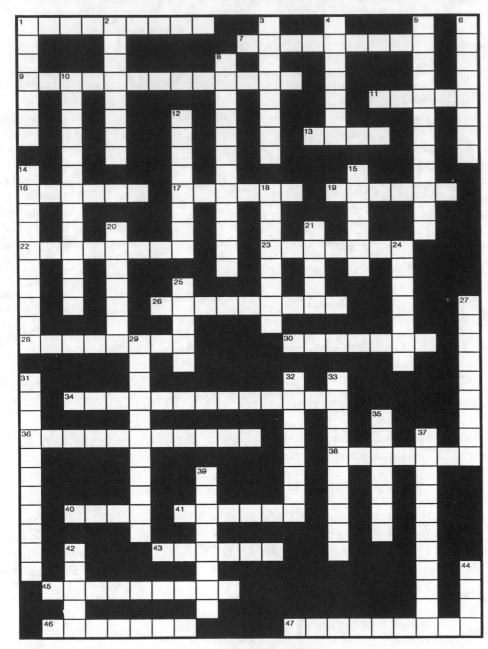

24

Across

1. This state borders Lake Michigan and is known for dairy products like cheese and ice cream.
7. This state's capital, Nashville, is the main center for country-western music.
9. This state was one of the first in our country, with famous historical places like Plymouth Rock and Boston.
11. Potatoes are the special farm crop in this state.
13. People will float and not sink in the great salt lake in this state.
16. The name of this state will make you think of Eskimos, igloos, and Husky dogs.
17. This state is nicknamed "the Sagebrush State," and its capital is Carson City.
19. A string of islands in the Pacific Ocean make up this state.
22. Chicago, which is called "the Windy City," is the biggest city in this state.
23. This state's nickname is "the Heart of Dixie," and its capital is Montgomery.
26. This northern state on the Atlantic coast shares borders with Pennsylvania, New York, and Delaware.
28. This is "the Cornhusker State," and its capital is named after a famous president.
30. This state has a name that sounds like "mountains" and is known for having mountains, forests, and national parks.
34. This state on the Atlantic coast has a capital called "Raleigh."
36. It is very cold in this northern state that borders Canada.
38. In this state you might see alligators, Mickey Mouse, and lots of people with suntans!
40. Virginia and ____ Virginia surround the Allegheny Mountains.
41. This northern state has the Pacific Ocean for a western border, where you can see large sand dunes and strong waves crashing against a rocky shore.
43. With 42-Down, this small state is sandwiched between Massachusetts and Connecticut.
45. In this state, the long Mississippi River comes through the famous city of New Orleans.
46. The busy city nicknamed "the Big Apple" shares the name of this state.
47. This southwestern state is named after the country on its southern border.

Down

1. Yellowstone National Park, where visitors can see mountains, forests, geysers, and sometimes bears, is in this state.
2. A state with an Indian name, "where the wind goes sweeping across the plains"; the capital city shares the state name.
3. A famous horse race, "the _____ Derby," takes place in this state.
4. A close neighbor to 5-Down, this small northern state is a good place to see fall colors in the autumn and to snow ski in the winter.
5. A next-door neighbor to 4-Down.
6. This state is known for its great city, St. Louis, called "the gateway to the West."
8. Philadelphia, "the city of brotherly love," is located in this large northeastern state.
10. The Atlantic coastal city Charleston is the capital of this state.
12. This state is the home of most of the beautiful Ozarks region.
14. This northwestern state is named after our first president.
15. Topeka is the capital of this state, and the farmers there grow wheat to supply bread for the U.S.A.
18. Right across the bay from New Jersey, this state is the smallest in the U.S.
20. "The Hoosier State" is directly southeast of Lake Michigan.
21. This state is the furthest northeast in the U.S.
24. This warm and dry state is the location of the Grand Canyon.
25. This state might make you think of cattle ranches and oil wells.
27. This state is known for having more than 10,000 lakes and is the home of the Twin Cities (Minneapolis and St. Paul).
29. Mt. Rushmore, the national monument honoring four presidents, is located in this state.
31. Hartford is the capital of this New England state.
32. Shaped like a large, lumpy mitten, this state has coasts along four of the Great Lakes.
33. This long, large state reaches all the way up to the redwood forests and all the way down to Mexico.
35. The beautiful and historic city of Atlanta is the capital of this southern state.
37. A long river with the same name forms the western border of this southern state.
39. Our nation's capital, Washington, D.C., is right next-door to this eastern state.
42. With 43-Across, this small state is sandwiched between Massachusetts and Connecticut.
44. This large midwestern state is just south of Michigan and Lake Erie.

Answers are on page 45.

Colors Along The Way

Keep your eyes open for things of all different colors—both inside and outside your car. Next to the colors listed below, list three things you see. Remember to look at vehicles, billboards, and inside your car. For example:

BLUE _____sky_____ _____car_____ _____jacket_____

BLACK _____ _____ _____

BLUE _____ _____ _____

BROWN _____ _____ _____

GOLD _____ _____ _____

GREEN _____ _____ _____

GREY _____ _____ _____

ORANGE _____ _____ _____

PINK _____ _____ _____

PURPLE _____ _____ _____

RED _____ _____ _____

SILVER _____ _____ _____

VIOLET _____ _____ _____

WHITE _____ _____ _____

YELLOW _____ _____ _____

You can pray:

Thank you, God, for all the many colors of our world. Thank you for making it beautiful for our eyes!

A Vacation in the Mountains

What colors and sights would you see on a vacation up in the mountains? Use your imagination to color this mountain scene.

For the LORD is the great God, the great King above all gods....
The mountain peaks belong to him. Psalm 95:3-4

What Am I?

A Guessing Game

Here's a game for you to play with one or more of the others traveling with you. The person holding the book is the clue-giver. Give one clue, then give each of the other players a chance to make a guess. If no one guesses the answer, give the second clue. Every player gets another chance to guess. Keep going until someone guesses the answer or you run out of clues.

---

1. What Am I?

Clue #1: You usually find me near water.
Clue #2: I am made up of billions and billions of smaller parts.
Clue #3: Wet or dry, I feel good under bare feet.
Clue #4: People use me to build castles and to scoop or bury.

---

2. What Am I?

Clue #1: I am tall and usually made of wood.
Clue #2: I stand outdoors.
Clue #3: My job has something to do with helping people communicate.
Clue #4: Long wires connect me to others just like me.

---

3. What Am I?

Clue #1: I am a small animal.
Clue #2: Sometimes I live outdoors, and sometimes I live indoors.
Clue #3: I often sing and sometimes even learn to talk.
Clue #4: My skin is covered with feathers and I like to live in a nest.

---

4. What Am I?

Clue #1: I help all kinds of people do all kinds of jobs.
Clue #2: I am a good organizer of information.
Clue #3: People use my letter keys and other buttons to make me do my job.
Clue #4: I usually have a screen called a monitor to help people work with me.

Answers are on page 45.

Add Them Up!

By now you're getting to be a great observer of all the things going on around you—both inside and outside of your car. Another fun travel game keeps track of various types of vehicles. You can play on your own or together with others in the car.

On Your Own

Set a time limit of about half an hour. Count how many of each type of vehicle you see. A good way to count is to make a slash for every item you see, like this | | | | . When you've got five items, make the fifth slash cross the others, like this ⧌ᵗᵗ. Ready? Get set. Go!

Semi-trucks _____

Buses _____

Mini-vans _____

Pickup trucks _____

Red cars _____

Blue cars _____

All Together

Play with another person (even the driver could play!), or split into two teams. Each side chooses one type of vehicle to watch for. One side might choose semi-trucks, and the other side might choose mini-vans. Or, one group could look for red vehicles, and the other for blue ones.

Set a time limit, then begin. Each team keeps count of the vehicles they see. Be sure to watch for vehicles in parking lots as well as for vehicles moving on the road. Whichever team has spotted the most vehicles at the end of the set time wins!

Praise the Creator!

Be a Praise Detective! Search these verses from the Bible for WHO is supposed to praise God. Make a list!

Praise the LORD from the earth,
*   you great sea creatures and all*
*   ocean depths,*
lightning and hail, snow and clouds,
*   stormy winds that do his bidding,*
you mountains and all hills,
*   fruit trees and all cedars,*
wild animals and cattle,
*   small creatures and flying birds,*
kings of the earth and all nations,
*   you princes and all rulers on earth,*
young men and maidens,
*   old men and children.*
Let them praise the name of the LORD,
*   for his name alone is exalted;*
*   his splendor is above the earth*
*   and the heavens.*
Psalm 148:7-13

_____   _____
_____   _____
_____   _____
_____   _____
_____   _____
_____   _____
_____   _____
_____   _____
_____   _____
_____

Who is the Creator of the world and of you? _____

Answers are on page 45.

What does it mean to "praise" God? Saying thank you to God is part of praising. But praising God also means saying out loud that God is great and wonderful for being who he is.

Use these spaces to write down words that describe God. Some examples are "faithful," "smart," or "kind."

_____   _____   _____

_____   _____   _____

Sing to the LORD a new song; sing to the LORD, all the earth.
Sing to the LORD, praise his name! Psalm 96:1-2

Make your own prayer of praise using the six describing words you just listed. Tell God that he is faithful, smart, kind, and all the good things you know about him.

Night Sky

Have you ever traveled at night? Or camped out in the forest—far from the city lights? The night sky is full of God's creations—the moon and the stars. Have you ever noticed the colors of a night sky? In the evening there are all the colors of sunset. And way into the night, the sky can look grey or deep blue or black. Use this page to draw a night sky.

O LORD, our Lord, how majestic is your name in all the earth! . . .
When I consider your heavens, the work of your fingers,
*   the moon and the stars, which you have set in place,*
what is man that you are mindful of him, the son of man that you care for him?
Psalm 8:1, 3-4

The writer of this psalm says that looking at the night sky reminds him how BIG God is and how small he seems. Do you feel small when you look at the night sky? Remember that God notices you—and he loves you!

God called the light "day," and the darkness he called "night." And there was evening, and there was morning—the first day. Genesis 1:5

On the Farm Super Search

Search for these words about animals and other things you might see on a farm vacation. Remember to read up and down, sideways, backwards, and diagonally!

acres
barley
barn
barnyard
bull
cat
chicken
chicken coop
chicks
corn
cow
cowbells
crops
dog
duck
ewe
farm
farmer
farmhouse
fence
fertilizer
fields
garden
gate
goose
grains
harvester
hay
haystack
heifer
hoe
horse
horseshoe

```
W  E  A  T  H  E  R  V  A  N  E  S  U  O  H  M  R  A  F
O  P  C  U  C  G  O  D  E  B  H  L  E  V  O  H  S  A  E
R  O  R  Y  H  I  T  U  G  A  A  O  H  O  R  H  O  M  R
R  E  E  P  I  T  C  S  Y  F  Y  T  E  F  S  A  B  I  T
A  W  S  I  C  O  A  R  D  I  S  J  A  Y  E  R  U  G  I
B  E  P  T  K  O  R  O  O  S  T  E  R  E  S  V  L  E  L
L  D  M  C  E  L  T  E  C  E  A  S  S  L  H  E  L  O  I
E  R  E  H  N  S  D  M  E  E  C  R  A  R  O  S  O  A  Z
E  A  S  F  C  C  O  R  N  D  K  O  V  A  E  T  P  T  E
H  Y  L  O  O  B  H  A  D  X  T  H  W  B  S  E  E  S  R
W  N  L  R  O  A  L  F  I  E  L  D  S  G  O  R  E  D  E
A  R  A  K  P  R  E  K  O  B  S  U  N  A  C  E  H  P  P
G  A  R  D  E  N  P  L  A  N  T  I  N  G  R  W  S  O  A
O  B  E  N  C  O  C  H  I  C  K  S  I  T  F  O  L  N  E
N  E  V  E  R  U  N  A  M  L  I  B  A  R  N  I  I  D  R
E  P  O  N  Y  M  O  P  I  A  T  G  O  O  S  E  A  B  E
K  I  T  C  H  E  N  M  L  M  T  A  D  U  C  K  P  A  T
C  G  R  A  I  N  S  A  O  B  E  N  Z  G  U  R  K  M  S
I  V  O  T  R  U  C  K  W  U  N  D  E  H  S  I  L  U  O
H  E  I  F  E  R  O  P  E  X  S  P  O  R  C  H  I  L  O
C  O  W  B  E  L  L  S  G  A  T  E  L  F  A  R  M  E  R
```

kitchen
kittens
lamb
loft
manure
milking stool
milkpail
mouse
mule
oats
overalls
pig
pitchfork
planting
pond
pony
reaper
rooster
rope
seed
shed
sheep
shovel
silo
tools
tractor
trees
trough
truck
wagon
weathervane
wheelbarrow

32

Answers are on page 45.

Tell a Silly Story

Use your creativity to make up a story using all the words listed below. You could:

1. Work together out loud with all the travelers in your car, taking turns in the storytelling. Illustrate your story on this page.

2. Write and illustrate the story on this page.

Things to include:

a hamburger

palm trees

a treasure chest

a shark

a race car

a treehouse

a boy named Marvin

a girl named Patty

an old man named Morty

After your story is told or written, give it an exciting title!

Next-Door Neighbors

Be a next-door neighbors detective! From the clues below, figure out the state names that belong in these groups of answers. For help, use the map in the middle of this book.

1. A northern pair of states with almost the same name. One is North and one is South.

_____

_____

2. Two southern states that are just north of Florida.

_____

_____

3. These northeastern states look like two triangles snuggled together.

_____

_____

4. Two states known for oil drilling. One is very large; the other looks like a kitchen pot with a long handle.

_____

_____

5. Three states that are side-by-side with names beginning with the letter "I."

_____

_____

_____

6. These side-by-side neighbors both border on Lake Superior.

_____

_____

7. These northwestern next-door neighbors share a mountainous border drawn as a squiggly line. One state is known for the potatoes that grow there.

_____

_____

8. These states, side-by-side just north of Mexico, look almost like squares.

_____

_____

9. An east-coast pair of states with almost the same name—one is North and one is South.

_____

_____

10. Lake Erie stretches along the north side of these three neighbors.

_____

_____

_____

11. These side-by-side states have Lake Michigan in between them.

_____

_____

12. One very long western state is right next door to a desert state.

_____

_____

13. These neighbors have almost the same name, but one is West.

_____

_____

14. The Ozarks begin in the south of one state, and are mostly in the north of the other.

_____

_____

Answers are on page 46.

34

Howdy, Partner!

Imagine the things you would do on a visit to a western ranch. Perhaps you'd watch a rodeo, learn to throw a lasso, ride a pony, shoot arrows at a target, and eat supper around a campfire. But a western vacation with no colors would be NO FUN! Put the fun into this picture using your crayons or markers.

Delicious Discoveries Super Search

Search this puzzle for some of your favorite things to eat. Remember to read up and down, sideways, backwards, and diagonally. And look out—searching this puzzle could make you VERY hungry!

```
S  T  R  A  W  B  E  R  R  Y  P  I  E  T  O  W  E  X  P
E  B  S  T  U  N  A  E  P  R  E  K  A  H  S  K  L  I  M
I  S  T  N  I  M  D  G  R  T  P  E  P  I  P  E  C  L  A
K  I  B  R  O  W  N  I  E  S  P  H  A  N  O  D  I  E  R
O  O  P  A  D  U  U  E  T  A  E  C  R  P  R  A  S  C  S
O  G  O  L  R  R  S  S  Z  P  R  N  T  E  D  N  P  I  H
C  U  P  C  A  K  E  S  E  H  O  A  E  S  M  O  O  U  M
P  T  I  H  T  Y  G  U  L  C  N  T  B  L  U  M  P  J  A
I  I  L  E  S  B  D  O  S  O  I  O  R  Y  G  E  E  T  L
H  L  L  W  U  C  U  M  C  N  P  F  E  S  D  L  I  H  L
C  P  O  I  C  A  F  A  A  I  I  R  H  H  L  N  C  A  O
E  S  L  N  D  R  T  L  R  O  Z  O  S  Y  D  S  A  C  W
T  A  O  G  S  A  O  T  A  N  Z  Z  B  R  U  N  R  C  S
A  N  B  G  T  M  H  I  M  R  A  E  V  E  M  I  A  R  E
L  A  R  U  U  E  O  C  E  I  A  N  M  G  U  S  M  A  I
O  N  O  M  N  L  T  E  L  N  C  Y  L  R  G  I  E  C  R
C  A  V  D  H  C  D  C  S  G  A  O  U  U  E  A  L  K  F
O  B  N  E  G  O  O  R  D  S  N  G  A  B  L  R  A  E  H
H  A  M  B  U  R  G  E  R  A  D  U  L  E  B  N  P  R  C
C  O  T  T  O  N  C  A  N  D  Y  R  O  S  B  R  P  J  N
C  A  K  E  D  E  H  M  F  U  R  T  C  E  U  O  L  A  E
F  U  D  G  E  N  A  C  H  O  S  L  A  E  B  C  E  C  R
E  S  O  D  A  E  P  O  T  A  T  O  C  H  I  P  S  K  F
I  W  S  N  O  C  O  N  E  S  F  E  O  C  S  O  C  A  T
P  U  D  D  I  N  G  E  C  I  R  O  C  I  L  P  K  O  L
```

Word list is on page 46.

Just Like a Tree

The Bible, God's Word, sometimes compares people to trees. Can you think of some ways a person and a tree are the same? The verses on this page will help you discover ways you can be like a strong and growing tree.

Praising the Creator

Let the fields be jubilant, and everything in them.
Then all the trees of the forest will sing for joy;
they will sing before the LORD, for he comes.
Psalm 96:12-13

You will go out in joy and be led forth in peace;
the mountains and hills will burst into song before you,
and all the trees of the field will clap their hands. . . .
This will be for the LORD's renown. Isaiah 55:12-13

These verses say that the trees will do two things. Search for the answers and write them here:_____   _____

These verses show that all of nature can praise God—just as people can praise God. Take time out right now to praise God—you can sing or clap your hands!

Tall and Strong and Full of Fruit

Blessed is the man who trusts in the LORD, whose confidence is in him.
He will be like a tree planted by the water that sends out its roots by the
*   stream.*
It does not fear when heat comes; its leaves are always green.
It has no worries in a year of drought and never fails to bear fruit.
Jeremiah 17:7-8

A tree is recognized by its fruit. Matthew 12:33

What do these verses say that trees need in order to grow and stay green?

What should a person do to be like a strong and growing tree?

_____   _____

The person who trusts in God grows tall and strong like a tree that is well nourished with water. A tree bears fruit, and that's how we know whether it is an apple tree or an orange tree or a lemon tree. How a person behaves shows us what type of person he or she is; that's what the verse means when it says "a tree is recognized by its fruit." Can people tell that you are part of God's family by the way that you behave?

I am like an olive tree flourishing in the house of God;
I trust in God's unfailing love for ever and ever. Psalm 52:8

Answers are on page 46.

Capital Crossword

Using the clues, fill in the blanks across and down with the names of state capitals. Use the map in the middle of this book to help you discover the answers. The capitals are listed to help you spell the words perfectly! (You won't use them all.)

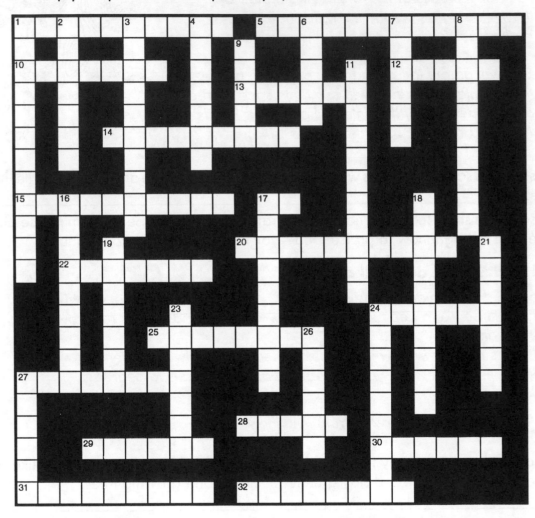

Albany	Charleston	Hartford	Madison	Richmond
Annapolis	Cheyenne	Helena	Montgomery	Sacramento
Atlanta	Columbia	Honolulu	Montpelier	St. Paul
Augusta	Columbus	Indianapolis	Nashville	Salem
Austin	Concord	Jackson	Oklahoma City	Salt Lake City
Baton Rouge	Denver	Jefferson City	Olympia	Santa Fe
Bismarck	Des Moines	Juneau	Phoenix	Springfield
Boise	Dover	Lansing	Pierre	Tallahassee
Boston	Frankfort	Lincoln	Providence	Topeka
Carson City	Harrisburg	Little Rock	Raleigh	Trenton

Answers on page 46.

Across

1. The capital of a large Pacific coast state.
5. Do you think "Indians" live here?
10. The capital of Michigan.
12. With 17-Across, the capital of New Mexico.
13. This capital begins with "Top."
14. These French words are the capital of Iowa.
15. This capital begins with a boy's name.
17. With 12-Across, the capital of New Mexico.
20. The capital of Pennsylvania.
22. This is Georgia's big city.
24. Though this sounds like a summer month, it's a wintery state.
25. This town begins with a sound like "heart."
27. The capital of North Dakota.
28. The capital of Oregon.
29. This capital is a woman's name.
30. This city is a twin to Minneapolis.
31. The capital of Tennessee and of country-western music.
32. The capital of Virginia.

Down

1. This capital has a "Lake" in the middle.
2. The capital of a tiny New England state.
3. The capital of Vermont.
4. New Jersey's capital.
6. This capital begins with the same letter as its state, Delaware.
7. The capital of the largest state.
8. You could say, "Small Stone."
9. _____ Rouge, Louisiana.
11. A long name with three sets of double letters.
16. This capital begins with a girl's name.
17. This capital name is also the name of a German city.
18. Nevada's state capital.
19. The capital of Washington.
21. This name sounds like an early autumn month.
23. The capital of Mississippi.
24. _____ City, Missouri.
26. Called "the mile-high city" because it's in Colorado's mountains.
27. A famous "Tea Party" took place in the harbor of this New England City.

WELCOME · TO · THE

AUSTIN

STATE OF TEXAS

Travel Log

A travel log is like a diary about a journey. Captains keep a daily log of what happens on their ship. You can keep a log of your vacation by making lists like this chart. A sample is given for you.

Today's Date	Where We Started	Things We Saw	Where We Stopped
6/12	Rockford, IL	road construction, the Mississippi River, 3 states	Minneapolis, MN
6/13	Minneapolis	capitol building, Lake Superior, Grandma	Duluth, MN
Today's Date	**Where We Started**	**Things We Saw**	**Where We Stopped**

Today's Date	Where We Started	Things We Saw	Where We Stopped

Devotions While You Travel

This time of travel could be a great time for you to share in a time of Bible exploration with the other travelers in your car. These devotional times can be long or short, depending on how much time you have to spend digging into God's Word. Here are some suggestions.*

WHO IS GOD?
(5 short devotions)

Devotional #1: *The Creator God*

Purpose

To focus on God as the Creator and controller of the world, and on people as God's good creation.

Explore

Genesis 1–2 Isaiah 40:25-26; 42:5-8
Psalm 139 Ephesians 1:4-6
Psalm 148 Colossians 1:15-20
  Revelation 4:9-11

Things to Do/Talk About

Name some of God's creations that you can see right now.

Name things that are special about you—one of God's good creations.

Draw some of your favorite things from God's creation, and make them into a booklet.

Sing

"He Owns the Cattle on a Thousand Hills"
"He's Everything to Me"
"I Love the Flowers"
any song that celebrates nature and creation

Pray

Thank God for his good creation, naming specific things you are thankful for.

Devotional #2: *The Sovereign God*

Purpose

To focus on how BIG God is—how powerful, loving, and awesome.

Explore

Exodus 15:1-18 Psalm 47
Psalm 9 Psalm 77:11-20
Psalm 24 Psalm 89:5-18
Psalm 29 Isaiah 40:10-31
Psalm 46:10 Revelation 15:1-4

Things to Do/Talk About

Make a list of words that describe God. For help, refer to the verses listed above.

Draw pictures of some of the biggest things you can think of (like elephants, the ocean, etc.). Remember that God is bigger than all of these things.

Sing

"How Great Thou Art"
"I Am So Glad That Jesus Loves Me"
"His Name Is Wonderful"
any song that praises God or gives him glory

Pray

Praise God in sentence prayers, taking turns among the travelers in your car (the driver can keep his eyes open!). Refer to your list of describing words.

42

*Based on devotions in chapter five, *Making Summer Count*, Joyce Heinrich and Annette LaPlaca, Shaw, 1991.

Devotional #3: *Jesus, the Savior*

Purpose

To explain God's gift of Jesus' life, death, and resurrection, and to understand God's plan of salvation.

Explore

Matthew 1:18-23	Romans 6:23
Mark 12:28-34	Ephesians 2:8-9
John 3:16-18	Titus 3:3-7
John 10:7-18	1 John 1:5-9
Romans 3:22-24	1 John 2:2
Romans 5:5-11	1 John 4:13-16

Things to Do/Talk About

Answer these questions together:

> Who can wash away sins?
> Who needs their sins washed away?
> When God comes into your heart and life, does he ever leave?
> Have you asked Jesus into your life?
> What does it mean to live for Jesus?

Make up a simple song as you travel that talks about Jesus taking away your sin.

Sing

"Stop—and Let Me Tell You"

"Into My Heart"

"Jesus, Jesus, Jesus"

any song about Jesus or salvation

Pray

Pray first for salvation, if you have not already accepted God's gift. Then pray for others who need Jesus.

Devotional #4: *The Holy Spirit*

Purpose

To realize that God's Holy Spirit is always with us.

Explore

Luke 11:9-13	2 Corinthians 3:17-18
John 14:25-27	Galatians 5:16-25
Acts 1:1-11; 2:1-4	Ephesians 1:13-14
Romans 8:5-16, 26-27	Ephesians 3:16-21
1 Corinthians 6:19-20	1 John 3:23-24
2 Corinthians 1:21-22	1 John 4:13-16

Things to Do/Talk About

Make a list of the things the Holy Spirit does as he lives in you. Refer to the Scriptures you've just read for help.

On a large sheet of paper, list the "Fruit of the Spirit" from Galatians 5:22-23. Then keep track of the way you treat other travelers in the car. Do your actions match the list you made?

Sing

"What a Friend We Have in Jesus"

"He Lives! He Lives!"

any song about the Holy Spirit or God being with you

Pray

Thank God for his Holy Spirit that will never leave you. Thank him for the Holy Spirit's help each day.

Devotional #5: *The Everlasting God*

Purpose

To focus on God as eternal and to remember that he will keep his promises forever.

Explore

Psalm 9:7-10	Psalm 145
Psalm 48:9-10, 14	Isaiah 26:3-4
Psalm 90:1-2	1 John 5:20
Psalm 103:17-19	Hebrews 1:8
Psalm 111	Hebrews 13:8
Psalm 136	Revelation 1:17-18

Things to Do/Talk About

Count how many times the phrase "His love endures forever" appears in Psalm 136.

Make a list of things Psalm 145 says about God or says that God will do.

Talk about how long forever is. Remember that as a child of God you will also live forever—in heaven with Christ.

Sing

"Coming Again"

"The Countdown's Getting Lower Every Day"

"Heaven Is a Wonderful Place"

any song about heaven or eternity

Pray

Praise God for being so awesome. Thank him again for his gift of eternal life.

Answer pages

Page 3 What to Take in the Car
1. maps 2. paper 3. crayons 4. books 5. pencils
6. garbage bag 7. snacks 8. toys 9. music
10. pillow 11. sunglasses 12. Bible 13. deck of
cards 14. notebook 15. camera

Page 3 Riddle
What's harder than following a road map? Folding it.

Page 5 On the Road Again

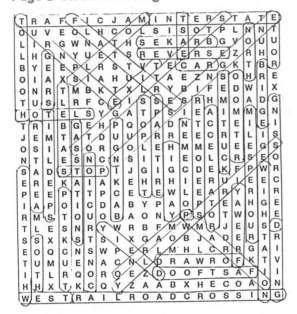

Page 6 Take It Along Crossword

Across
1. coat
3. games
5. music
7. backpack
9. jeans
10. flashlight
12. pillow
13. sneakers
14. toys

Down
1. camera
2. umbrella
4. map
6. sunglasses
8. comic books
11. snacks

Page 10 Who Am I? A Guessing Game
1. A road construction worker
2. A schoolbus driver
3. A nurse or doctor
4. A baker

Page 15 Riddle
What kind of music do fathers sing in the car? Pop
music.

Page 17 God the Provider
God provides for: ravines, mountains, beasts of the
field, wild donkeys, birds, earth, grass, man.

Page 19 Take a Trip

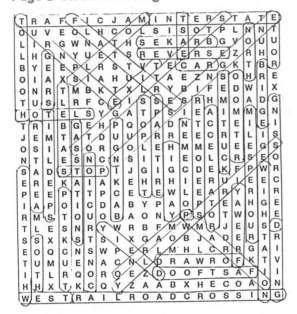

Page 20 Riddle
What ten-letter word starts with g-a-s? Automobile.

Page 21 Match Them Up!
sandcastle building——LAKE or OCEAN/BEACH
flying kites——PARK
waterskiing——LAKE or OCEAN/BEACH
sledding——PARK or MOUNTAIN/WOODS
camping——LAKE, MOUNTAIN/WOODS, PARK,
OCEAN/BEACH
feeding seagulls——OCEAN/BEACH
rollerskating——PARK
surfing——OCEAN/BEACH
whale-watching——OCEAN/BEACH
jogging——PARK or OCEAN/BEACH
swimming——LAKE or OCEAN/BEACH
fishing——LAKE or OCEAN/BEACH
ferris-wheel riding——AMUSEMENT PARK

shell collecting——OCEAN/BEACH
snorkeling——LAKE or OCEAN/BEACH
picnicking——LAKE, MOUNTAINS/WOODS,
   PARK, OCEAN/BEACH
rollercoaster riding——AMUSEMENT PARK
hiking——MOUNTAINS/WOODS
boating——LAKE or OCEAN/BEACH
diving——LAKE or OCEAN/BEACH
merry-go-round riding——AMUSEMENT PARK

3. Kentucky
4. Vermont
5. New Hampshire
6. Missouri
8. Pennsylvania
10. South Carolina
12. Arkansas
14. Washington
15. Kansas
18. Delaware
20. Indiana
21. Maine

24. Arizona
25. Texas
27. Minnesota
29. South Dakota
31. Connecticut
32. Michigan
33. California
35. Georgia
37. Mississippi
39. Maryland
42. Rhode (Island)
44. Ohio

Page 28 What Am I? A Guessing Game
1. Sand
2. A telephone pole
3. A bird
4. A computer

Page 30 Praise the Creator
Who should praise God: sea creatures, ocean depths, lightning, hail, snow, clouds, stormy winds, mountains, hills, fruit trees, cedars, wild animals, cattle, small creatures, birds, kings, nations, princes, rulers, young men, maidens, old men, children.
The Creator of the world and of you: God.

Page 32 On the Farm Super Search

Pages 24-25 50 States Super Crossword
Across
1. Wisconsin
7. Tennessee
9. Massachusetts
11. Idaho
13. Utah
16. Alaska
17. Nevada
19. Hawaii
22. Illinois
23. Alabama
26. New Jersey
28. Nebraska
30. Montana
34. North Carolina
36. North Dakota
38. Florida
40. West (Virginia)
41. Oregon
43. (Rhode) Island
45. Louisiana
46. New York
47. New Mexico

Down
1. Wyoming
2. Oklahoma

45

Page 34 Next-Door Neighbors
1. North Dakota, South Dakota
2. Alabama, Georgia
3. Vermont, New Hampshire
4. Texas, Oklahoma
5. Iowa, Illinois, Indiana
6. Minnesota, Wisconsin
7. Idaho, Montana
8. Arizona, New Mexico
9. North Carolina, South Carolina
10. Ohio, Pennsylvania, New York
11. Wisconsin, Michigan
12. California, Nevada
13. West Virginia, Virginia
14. Missouri, Arkansas

Page 36 Delicious Discoveries Word List

banana split	jelly beans
brownies	juice
bubble gum	lemonade
cake	licorice
candy	lollipop
candy bar	malt
caramel apples	marshmallows
caramel corn	milkshake
caramels	mints
cheeseburger	mousse
chewing gum	nachos
chocolate-chip	onion rings
cookies	pastry
Coca-cola	peanuts
cotton candy	pepperoni pizza
crackerjack	pie
cupcakes	popcorn
custard	popsicle
doughnuts	potato chips
french fries	pretzels
frozen yogurt	pudding
fudge	raisins
gumdrops	sherbet
hamburger	sno-cones
hot dog	soda
hot fudge sundae	strawberry pie
ice cream cone	tacos

Page 38 Capital Crossword

Across	Down
1. Sacramento	1. Salt Lake City
5. Indianapolis	2. Concord
10. Lansing	3. Montpelier
12. Santa	4. Trenton
13. Topeka	6. Dover
14. Des Moines	7. Austin
15. Charleston	8. Little Rock
17. Fe	9. Baton (Rouge)
20. Harrisburg	11. Tallahassee
22. Atlanta	16. Annapolis
24. Juneau	17. Frankfort
25. Hartford	18. Carson City
27. Bismarck	19. Olympia
28. Salem	21. Augusta
29. Helena	23. Jackson
30. St. Paul	24. Jefferson
31. Nashville	26. Denver
32. Richmond	27. Boston

Page 37 Just Like a Tree
The trees will: 1. sing for joy 2. clap their hands.
What trees need: Water.
What a person should do: Trust in the Lord.